*Black silhouetted mountain
cracked on dark horizon—
    full moon lights my way.*

Say No More

*Poetry from the Back Roads and Blue Highways of America—
and the Adventures of the Interstellar Roadside Prophet*

Gregory O'Toole

© Rhythm Mountain Studios 2001
www.rmsart.com

Copywrite © 2001 by Gregory O'Toole and Rhythm Mountain Studios (RMS)
Chicago. Missoula. Rico.

All rights reserved under International Copywrite Conventions. Except for brief passages quoted in a newspaper, magazine, radio, or television review, no part of this book may be reprinted in any form without permission of the author and Rhythm Mountain Studios.

ACKNOWLEDGMENTS

Parts of this book originally printed in the *Telluride Daily Planet*. Grateful acknowledgment is made to Central Plains Books, Winfield, Kansas.

Publisher's Cataloging-in-Publication
(Provided by Quality Books, Inc.)

O'Toole, Gregory.
  Say no more : poetry from the backroads and blue highways of America, and the adventures of the Interstellar Roadside Prophet / Gregory O'Toole. -- 1st ed.
   p. cm.
   Includes index.
   ISBN 0-9711125-0-9

   I. Title.

PS3565.T67S39 2001   811'.6
                           QBI01-700764

"——I'd first left home with a second hand tent and worn out backpack, several years before on a few short wanderings out west that began a process I could no longer control. I had learned the way of the road, the honesty in the road, to trust in the road—and those along it. From now on I would be a traveler—inexorable curiosity for new discovery—seeking out a place for myself which always seemed further on—always further, and at the same time, always toward home———"

Noah Dempsey, *the String Cheese Diaries*

Contents

Like an Elephant in the Forest *poems from the old southwest*

Think Sunrise	3
White Room New Mexico Sand Dune Blues	4
In God's Country	6
Broke–down Deserted	8
The Voice of the New Generation	9
Big City Lights Painter	11
From Out of Chicago	13
Weminuche Wilderness	14
Old Joe Apparently	16
Brick Layer Poet	17
The Way I See My Girl and Out Into the Sun	18
Strong Southern Wind	20

Autobiography of A Wolf *poems like slow–falling rain*

Another Marathon	25
Walking in the City	26
Twelve Stories Concrete	28
34 South Wabash	29
What I Do	31
The Real Revolution	33
Mission Mountain Love Poem	34
Country Donuts Buddhist Poem	36

v

Some Things Take You Higher *poems from the journey home*

A Long Time—A Letter To My Friend	39
Clayton Delaney	45
I Met Edward Abbey Reincarnated As A Horse	46
Absolute Liberation	48
Eventual List Poem	50
Montana Meditation Sounds	52
Coffee Shop Mantra	54
Idaho	57

this very being is *It*.

West Coast Rhythms	61
Rocky Mountain Sidewalk Sutra	64
Afternoon Sunset America	66
Those Cosmic Companions	68
Don't Want To	75
Sun Dried Tomato	79
Barefoot Mountain	83
Why I Walk *(for Cassidy)*	84
Princess Suede Black	89
Apartment Poem	91
A Day in the Life	92

Early January Mountain Morning Frost

Jesus Bread Sandwich	99

Bukowski and the West	100
Four Foot Snow	101
Midnight Capital Limited	103
Time Travel Train	104
Unemployed	105
Mountain Girl	106
Randolph Street	107

Far Off Places

Here Fly	111
Daikensho Days	112
The Big Question	113
Warhol's Number	114
Route 200 East	115
4WD	116
Double Door Inn	117

Daikensho in the City, Daikensho in the Woods

1633 N Damen Ave	121

American Road Prose & Highway Dharma

The Year I Changed the Royal Guard	125
Remembered	132

Western Haiku 133

A fine and kind dedication—

Irwin Allen Ginsberg—
2 a.m. June 3, 1926
Beth Israel Hospital
Newark, New Jersey—

and forever.

To *those cosmic companions*—Joe, my family, U.B., Sunshine
Lauren, Mike, the Montana folks—my drunken wood–cuttin'
neighbor and his drunken flower–plantin' girl, Canoe Ken, the
river rat, Beethoven lady across the street, Jerry Blackfoot
Indian asleep on my floor, Cai Bristol, Kailash Dharma Center,
Jack Castor's caboose on the mountain—whiskey old man,
Casey from Memphis spinning records and saving the planet,
all those cats on my Missoula porch, and guitar–pickin' Patrick,
walkin' boss beatnik from old Virginy——

    and Cassidy—
      struttin' howl like lone grey wolf
     right
       down
         to the sea.

Say No More

Like an Elephant in the Forest
poems from the old southwest

Think Sunrise

Think big, think long, think long–term
Think short–term and Now!
Think daily, think custom, think your way through the day
Think time, think time out
Think today and for tomorrow
        never coming back.
Think sun times,
        think moon times—
        think hard times ain't never gunna change.
Think sunrise, new day—great golden landscapes in newborn
        horizon—infant to grandfather space.
Think coast–side, seaside, and shipwrecked seagulls
        hovering infinity in salty raintime midnight air.

Think road–worn and pacified—
Think stubborn and calm—
Think often, laconic and still,
        like old man meditation
        in my dusty southwest American dawn——

Think barefoot—left on the curb like inner city youth
        standing on the heels of rock and roll—
        three–hundred stories crumbling madness in NYC,

        daylight starvation in a globalized world.

o4.o1

White Room New Mexico Sand Dune Blues

White truck border patrol mexican man says go
        and pass through Soapdish Yucca barbed wire fences
High Stealth bomber sonic breakthrough
        vibrating hills of sand
        a quiet radar in my mind.

Eighty–seven mph convertible rag top mission
        sandstone Texas—New Mexico border lights on the run
        green gold differential high hat motor–on
        to Alamagordo broke–down buses
        beat down and rusting in ten—year shanty town
            roadside dust.

My life is small enough
        to pack up everything I own
        and find my way home,
        driving all the time right back to you.

I am somewhere between the Vidyadhara, a Buddhist monk—
        William Blake, visionary—
        and lost American transient
        sitting cross–legged and firm
        in the early southwest springtime,
        sleeping on wet leaves,
        tying on my shoes in the infant dawn
        new morning mist—

        old Rocky Mountain freight train on my mind.

My life is small enough
        to pack up everything I own
        and find my way home,
        driving all the time right back to you.

Off through the trees the silver barrel commuter train
        sounds its whistle
        and clicks slowly steadily on,
        like old man winter come and gone,

rocking back and forth down the tracks.

Where you off to? I say

We can have nightlife drinks in old leaky open air bar
       under the train tracks—
       middle Wicker Park in early springtime rain.

My life is small enough
       to pack up everything I own
       and find my way home,
       driving all the time right back to you.

When I'm really rich and old I'll be a snob—
       order grand obnoxious playthings
       and the finest white wine just to have it.
       then smash it on a cliff like Big Sur
       or give it to my Dad and laugh

If I go to jail I'll go to a penitentiary,
       not a state penitentiary,
       but the psychiatric ward pumped full of knockout drugs
       running circles in the courtyard.

       visitors every Sunday with scrambled eggs
              and maple syrup
       writing new–born wild fictionpoems sitting
              cross–legged park bench
       with the rest of the blue collar loones

       no more white collar tunes

       just stark white pajamas,
       Andy Kaufman hairdos,
       and a big fat notebook for the stars.

o5.o1 Chicago

> *This hit me, starting out a couple weeks ago, sitting in Flippers bar in Missoula, Montana where I was the only patron— just me and old lady bartender and the fires. Always the fires. Mind if I change the channel? I asked her. She couldn't care less— and upon flipping a couple times I came across A&E's* Biography— *they played Bob Dylan's twice. So there I sat— and here you go.*

In Gods Country

Play for me a hobo song of love
        so full of grace
Shine on me red harvest moon
        and something I can chase
I'll play for you a magic poem
        and ramblings from my mind—
Rocky Mountain midnight blues,
        come back and you will find

> *Bluegrass in the mountain towns*
> *Dharma in the hills,*
> *Midwest prairies endless gold—*
> *Southern whiskey stills*

Mission Mountains rising fast
        runnin' cross the land
Rise up now to see that sky
        your own life in your hand.

For now it's told with looks of old—
        a dewdrop on the grass
Southwest sun, new mountain town
        fighting time to pass

> *Bluegrass in the mountain towns*
> *Dharma in the hills,*
> *Midwest prairies endless gold—*
> *Southern whiskey stills*

Been around some southern towns
        and west Montana heights—
Summit reaching,
        Old man preaching,
        Alaskan Northern Lights

Holy southwest silent road,
        Walking Saints in time—
Dhammapada dusty suits
        in meditation mind

        Bluegrass in the mountain towns
        Dharma in the hills,
        Midwest prairies endless gold—
        Southern whiskey stills

Play for me a hobo song with love
        so full of grace
Shine on me red harvest moon
        and something I can chase—
I'll play for you a magic poem
        and ramblings from my mind—
Rocky Mountain midnight blues,
        come back and you will find

        Bluegrass in the mountain towns
        Dharma in the hills
        Midwest prairies endless gold
        Southern whiskey stills

09.00 Durango, CO

Broke–down Deserted

I could find the inspiration in a dead truck on the side of the road—
      its story flashing brightly
        to anyone who cares to see it

I could find the rhythm in a leaky faucet cracked and rusted—
      New England mansion
      or skid row shanty
      and dance to it under the moon

I could find the muse in giant azure–blue eyes behind wire rim glasses
      for fourteen–day epic poems
      or Nowhere's–ville broke–down roadside tragedy
      and sit silent in the sun

I would much rather enjoy this grandeur
      of honest grays and deep dark greens
      and browns and sacred blues
      than pay a dollar for a train ride through the city

The sun brings out the rusted iron greens
      and soon–September oranges and reds
      shining in my holy southwest sun
      above the cool blue highways I dreamt about when I was nine

Though I suppose it selfish to complain
      as summer must enjoy its wealth while it is here

      demanding clutter and perspiration I do not feel like madness

Do not stumble upon that weary road—
      In my mind there are no weary roads

      five dollars will take it everywhere from here and

      never
      let
      go.

08.31.00 Durango, CO

The Voice of the New Generation

I saw one white flash play chess on my horizon
Saw one grey wolf play balance by the sea—
    I play black cloak mysteries
    in ancient manor castles,
    cracked mortar
    and degrading in the sand.

Wild gelatin flowers and Chicago cityscape—
    dancing shadows on my dash
    keep the engine alive and at full boar
    like renaissance king dharma lion,
    roaring down the highway
        reminding me I'll be back around soon

Still as born again mantra
    wet from the rain,
    singing in the snowfall late December—
    found God in the broken streets
    from morning till 2 a.m.
    wild in the night—

    shining in the sun.

It's the role of landscape as a symbol
    of cosmic structure and process, they say

I soon realized the ethical revolution
    as I stared four hundred miles into the rusted out bumper
    and dust covered ten–year–old license plate
    of a baby blue nineteen sixty–eight
    Ford flareside pickup

As myself and the medieval army of twisted road machines
    and hi–fired mystics
    overtook Iowa then Nebraska
    and the entire midwestern United States for that matter
    in a harrowing cloud of chaos and disorder.

    Chrome handlebars and over packed half–tons
    shined bright on my horizon

"You jumped the gun" they told me—

but there were no guns to be seen—

just wild pounding rhythmic heartbeats
and starry constellations in our midnight sky.

Renaissance bearded lunatics
    run amuck through cornfields—

    Did you know, I asked them,
    that there's an entire social class in this country
    made up of educated jack–asses
        in foofy bubble gum SUV's
        and bourgeoisie–synthetic mail order
        bullet proof underwear?

    where right mindfulness and right action
        give way to diamond ring fingers
        and freebox cashmere sweaters.

It's an ethical revolution I've popped the top on—
    A revolution of the intelligent one's
        the alive one's
        the Awake one's
        the aware one's
        the REAL one's—

All this, I say, from the bottle wrapper pen marks
    worn and salty from the sea,
    tired and jaded from cross country cigarettes,
    new–born and alive from southern barstools and
        southwest shambhala nights
        and Appalachian flights—

All this, I say, from afternoon vagabond
    riding high in two wheel drive
    automatic southwest sun.

o1.12.o1 Rico, CO

Big City Lights Painter

Big city painter—
       my god, there's something so grand about it—
           and complex.

          Do you know?..
Traditional formal–istic romance on canvas.
Crumbling decrepit elevated subway tracks.

I'll buy a t–shirt with Allen Ginsberg's face on it
and wear it till it falls apart
shredded and worn off the bones in my back.

Reserve a seat in the theatre rows
fold–down velvet lounge chairs
       beginning act one.

Here's where the scene begins
      —or began four years today

       with the naked angels running in the streets
       and the Great Walking Saints
       for fast–paced America
       midwest–mountain liberation.

I had a vision at six a.m. this morning
    as the foggy rain kept a beat on the roof
    and outside cried tears on the windowsill.

I had a vision of a grand ballroom gallery,
    flawless bleach white walls,
    twenty–five foot ceilings—
        and the crowd that came to see.

My crowd was old jaded poets
    in work boot army coats
    drinking wine and talking about the world
       and film.

My crowd was two shining Buddhist monks
       in formal saffron robes
       smiling and taken aback by the colors on the walls.

My crowd was delta girls sunburnt and shining
       from bayou afternoons
       and back porch dulcimer moonshine
       back to the city one more time

My crowd was rich and poor and dancing in the alley.

Mystic long haired wandering white man
       strolling along with his dog
       or through the Cascades of western Washington
       and Mount Rainier
              alone five days
              high as a kite
              high as the sun

              to walk five days in the city
              or just to see my show.

Big city lights painter—
       there's something so grand about it—
            and complex—

            Do you know?

05.oo Chicago

From Out of Chicago

Outerspace Sanskrit writing dialog in my head
Me with my vacuum
       and you in your diamond ring finger
       lost in the desert
       and saguaro sand dunes
       running languid to the horizon.

Started out homeless and back to the cities rainy day blacktop
       streets with holes
       cowering roles
       of tire tracks in the alleys.

Feels like weeks since Rico Hobo Club
       since bonfires in December nights,
            drunk indians on cardboard
      and me in patchwork Lazy–boy
           sitting crowned like a king
           and highrise mermaids
           drinking cold beer
           in warm September nights.

Weeks since Rocky Mountain springtime
       since summertime parkinglots
           trailblazing campgrounds
           burning insight all around.

Weeks since agave southwest autumn
       since indian summer
           October New Mexico
           Navajos pouring sand across my feet
           sweating in the lodge.

It's like singing in ancient Mexico catholic church
       or sitting west Montana meditation
       and silent sunshine coffee house window

       warm on the inside, cold on the out.

chicago 02.01

Weminuche Wilderness

I like piano key bones shining new
        or rotting porcelain in the attic—
        an ivory muse inside my head.

I like jaded mountain trails
        run south along Old Epic Ridge
        and the late afternoon bees buzzing
            quiet on my feet.

I like the river—
I like the rocks below crashing white
        water falls in Vallecito sun.

I like the road

I like the rain

I like old age stovetop hot chocolate
        in late night Rocky Mountain campfires
        and giant maple syrup mugs
        from the cabin over Schofield Pass.

I am in the wind

I am in the sun—

I am matchstick oil paint in big city Chicago
        and Abbey–town southwest

I am a drink of water last
        two hundred miles of trail

I am Jack Micheline, starry–eyed mystic sadhu
        singing William Blake lyrics

        free in cold mountain rhythmic population
        free in deep–mind holy meditation
        free in verse of the San Juan eagle—
            never stop soaring
            in my sacred harvest moon
            southwest Colorado night.

I am giant cedar jester old man
    towering four hundred years—
    el communicado of the forest—

    sending smoke signals to Oregon
    and reaching for the moon.

I am born again mantra
    wet from the rain—
    found God in the trees
    In midnight September
        magic
        motion
        streams.

o9.oo Durango

Old Joe Apparently

Old Joe, apparently I've just come across
        the perfect rhinestone nightmare

    with girls above in
    high heeled massacres

    come from the place where
        mountains and roads go on forever

    wearing eye liner purple on TV
    cowboy boots fringed at the heel
        outta sidewalk sundayshop windows
        laced in amphetamines
        and freeze tag coul de sac glowstick games

        tin foil shoulder straps
        baked at four hundred degrees

I'll go to the desert tomorrow
    in half moon fantastic leather
    rolled out in Columbia sandstone fantasies
        born real in the sun

    or else change my reasons
    and run wild in the night—

    two shoes on my feet
    and nothing,
        nothing but matchstick lamp posts
        and my mystic mountain sunrise

        on
        my
        mind.

09.07.00 Durango

Brick Layer Poet

I am brick layer poet
        wild hair Southwest
        mid–morning army coat blues

Bricks make my words—
        complex octagon wedged tight in a row
        simple squares cut sharp and my fingers bleed

Cool mountain air
        Navajo man pounding sand
        terra firma—
        table mesa hot stove kiln in
            old Mexico

            one day
            away.

o9.oo Durango

The Way I See My Girl and Out Into the Sun

I walk across the desert flats to watch you from afar
    soft music sounds
      to echo back a voice from my guitar

      in wild stampeding midnight city streets—
      in old world Delicate Arch snowfalls—
      in lost holiday swerving mountain roads
          too gone in thought
          too wrapped in sight
          too tired to focus on broken painted
          highway lines

I see old–school angel–eye reading glasses
    and dreadlock back pocket poetry books

      stacked high like sculpted pyramids
      to dangle fingers in the clouds.

I see ancient shambhala spirits run wild cross the sand
    a spinning sunrise minstrel
    like holy Mount Zion windmills
        with nothing in your hands.

I see sunburnt sandstone churches
    with last–century crucifixes casting shadows to your side—

    I see your eyes open wide.

Run ramped high speed marathons
    through Vallecito fog at twilight
Run smooth sailing slick engine races
    across early morning crystal clear deserts
        to bathe in the river
        to sleep in the wild

        and find peace at your side in my mind.

Like a renaissance stone mason cathedral
built handmade and strong
standing proud in San Miguel storms

Like a wondrous spirit gypsy
    sitting quiet in my truck
        or dancing in the isles
    wandering beyond the interior walls
        and Rocky Mountain meditation halls

I see you standing there like one last leaf in late autumn branches
    and floating in the wind—
    twirling in the air,

    shining in the sun.

11.oo Rico (for Lauren)

Strong Southern Wind

And my only concern was positioning my notebook
        in the yellow street lamp glow
        between the erie shadows
                of naked tree limbs
                and the truck door swung open wide

The train cars ten feet away—
        broke–down rusted of the old Santa Fe line
        played backdrop to the theatre play in my head
                and on the streets in front of my eyes.

Where you off to? I asked—

Silent old man boxcar
        with his faded SF initials stenciled
        on his side said nothing out loud

                but sat silent
                and let out one more exhausted
                        steel rail sigh.

I know, I thought, I understand—

        I sometimes feel that way
        after walking twenty miles
        in beat–down laced–up boots
        on the trail to sit silent meditation
                on the rocks above the gorge

And on the sunshine days,
        quite golden in the sun
        I have no water in my pack
                and drink from the river
                at the base of where I sit

        Or walk on silent
                Like giant brown buffalo,
                Like an elephant in the forest.

        There is a strong wind that blows thru here
        up from the South
        where natives squat in the dirt

and drink wine in wicker baskets—

old holy women dried up and brown
      crushing cornmeal
      weaving ancient Navajo rugs

Sage brush bouncing on the Ute reservation
      up from the South

      bottomed–out pick–ups
      with newspapers yellow from
            nineteen sixty–three.

Just one more day I said that old road with faded center lines
      and bullet hole signs
      will stay where it's at.

      I'll whistle down that road headed west
      in the early mountain dawn
      of morning.

09.oo Durango

Autobiography of A Wolf
poems like slow-falling rain

Another Marathon

Last night I saw Gary Snyder in my bed
       sitting indian style
       like you did when you were ten
       like a snowstorm blizzard
          in stark white
             East Indian Chogyam Trungpa pajamas,
      short cropped head of hair
      graying bearded sage

     and nothing on his mind.

This morning I woke up
      with muddy old running shoes
          tied to my feet
          from two days in the forest
          after rainfall marathon
          January sunshine—

     a torn and beaten—
     freshly written book of mantras

          by my side.

1.1o.oo Chicago

Walking in the City

It's living ten months in Rocky Mountain log cabin Colorado,
Nine months space station Mission Range Montana
    and everywhere in between.

    Jump back turn around west Loop Chicago—

        downtown skyscrapers
        and the Art Institute
        to study painting four years
        and meditate in Bucktown
        till it's late and the sun goes down—

It's what made Jack Kerouac split,
    head back to Lowell, Mass.
    with a twenty pound typewriter
    like a Catholic priest
    no attachments or expensive cars—
        to get right down to It.

It's Allen Ginsberg on the edge
    holy bearded east indian
    Chogyam Trungpa western Buddhist,
    Dharma Lion mastodon backbone
        the ring leader of one grand show.

It's smokey pint beer
    at dim red bar smalltown Illinois or in the city,
    and all the while feeling the same.
It's redheads drinking coffee that makes your mind go numb
It's sixteen inch tires on an old pickup truck
It's the Cedar Bar painters,
    NYC nineteen fifties abstract expressionists

It's a harvest moon.

It's four feet of snow anywhere in the world at midnight
It's pawprints on the carpet,

It's oil paint and turpentine and Wrangler jeans
    you stopped watching out for a long time ago—

It's fifty states—
>	it's America,
>	it's red, white and blue—crimson and indigo—
>	and all the two–lane
>	dusty town highways in between.

02.18.00 Chicago

Twelve Stories Concrete

Saturday is the best place to be
    sitting twelve stories up
    to where I took the elevator,
        or walked an infantry of stairs
        of molded concrete to my couch
        that's old
        and dusty—
        brown, found in a Salvation Army thriftstore alley,

        like I'd have in a small big city apartment
        or New Mexico porch
            —for a place to sit and think
            or read
            and talk to visitors late night by the moon.

    A hundred and seventy–five feet off the ground—
        off the street—the concrete
        at twelve stories up.

It's peaceful up here
        and the city doesn't make a sound.
I hear a refrigerator hum in the next room.

The people all look like ants,
        nobody can talk from up here,
no cars can sound their horn,
        angry and calling names,
jackhammers secretly crack open sidewalk cement,

traffic policeman's whistle doesn't blow—
    the tugboats have cotton in their ears.

I can look out over the water,
        azure blue, quiet as a church

        —refrigerator humming,
        brown couch lounging
        at twelve
        stories
        up.

02.04.00 SAIC Michigan Building

34 South Wabash

I had a meeting on Wabash Street
    with a person I did not know.

Just pop in
    twelve blocks of frigid January wind
    and a dollar-
    equals one hour-
    in the meter

        sticky coins don't work,
        just make things worse;
        throw them in the snow
        and leave them
        where some bum can buy french fries
            or cigarettes
            come spring.

Steno-notebook receptionist girl
shuffles me in,
    chewing her pencil
        under Andy Warhol glasses
            circa 1959.

asks me my name three times
    down the hall
    mispronounces her co-workers name,

He's my good friend she tells me–
    I smile and nod.
    Shaking my head inside.

She's my good friend he tells me
    about receptionist girl
        I laugh, but he doesn't know why.

Sit in the brown chair
    Under his lamp

        that just reeked of
        gaudy pink femininity,
    and dainty little girl department store cheapness.

    The fake pearls are what made it.

Tight black Jim Morrison leathers
        cut short with bobby socks or stelletto heals
        with long sleeve red lingerie
            under his top shirt
            he lisped and frollocked
            for forty eight minutes
                about what makes him happy
                about computers

                and what color does to the economy

    I dozed off, like I was on the nod,
        he didn't notice.
    On and on he went—
        A man possessed,
        or a woman possessed—

    I think I threw up
    and went home.

o1.19.oo Chicago

What I Do

Because that's what I do I said

What is what you do? she asked
        wrinkling forehead
        and twinkling eyes—

        Come up with ideas,
        I have them all the time

                —it's what I do.

    Sometimes I have ideas and write about them
    Sometimes I have ideas and paint about them

    Sometimes I dwell on them
            like an old, drunk bum
            with watery red eyes on the alligator
            bayou banks of New Orleans—
                    who hasn't moved for days

    Sometimes I have ideas and shout about them
            or talk nonstop for hours about them—

        and sometimes don't say a word.

    Sometimes I laugh about them
            or people laugh at me about them
            or laugh with me about them
            or don't laugh at all

    Sometimes I make dinner about them
    Sometimes I go hungry about them

    Sometimes drive cross–country
            forty–eight states about them
            and sometimes never leave home

    Sometimes get payed about them
            or meditate in Montana gompa about them

    Sometimes I fall in love from them

                or think its love
                and end up lonely—

        but sometimes I know it's love
                because I can see it in her eyes
                        like a tired midnight celestine
                        in heavenly black silk

I turn into the holy sun
                warm rising with the dawn
                misty cold winter mornings

                        and never
                        come
                        down.

02.03.00 Chicago

The Real Revolution

Vino worldwide noWhere diva—
    a byway—
    a forest.

High road in frio coast—
    a madman on the loose.

Off to a cottage—
    Ginsberg and
    ninety sangha bears.

Paperback revolution
    in cottonwood fields or
    languid barstool gingerman afternoons

    this may well be, I say
    the last great rainforest in the city

    for raincoat prophets—
        barefoot and wise

    on southbound train tracks
        and azure skies.

    for matchbook glass bottles
        cracked on wartime streets

    for ancient frangelico barmaids

    for highwire walkers in cowboy boots at dawn

    for midtown computer generation lost youth
        found in the sunshine alleyways

        and high mountain valley—ways
        with nothing but a dollar in their pockets,
        the packs on their backs—

        and fast–paced ECO–world domination
        on their minds.

06.29.00 Chicago

Mission Mountain Love Poem

Mission Mountains
      snow–capped high rockies
      western montana royal dinosaurs,

You sit golden in the sun
      for three years now in my mind
      and in my heart.
I'll come back to you today
      and again forever.
I'll leave you today, again,
      and come back again forever.

If you went away
      I'd have a funeral service for you
      and the way you make me feel

      Buried deep Inside,
      I'd see it through watery eyes,
      and feel my new broken heart
           slowly healing now
           and again.

I never knew I would see you
      or meet you
      let alone, fall in love with you.
      But only in the West.

Towering black castles,
      royal dinosaurs
      reaching for big sky
      or open casket funeral house blues

      always inviting to leave here,
      rest in your arms
      or sit by your side
      and fall asleep each night with you—
           quiet content silence
           contemplating the stars over head
           and what's Inside.

Alter–shrine in one Grand churchyard
    Soto Zen zafu posture,

        You make me feel complete
        when I don't feel completely alone
            and safe
        in the mystic Holy mountain ranges

        and dusted–red rock formations
            of my home

        in America.

09.04.00 Montana

Country Donuts Buddhist Poem

I saw the world today—
    or my world anyway—
    in the half eaten remains of a
        crumbled peanut donut
        on the counter of a diner
        that wasn't even mine—

Maybe it was in the blue jeans
    torn and beaten
    or the wrinkled years in the face sitting content
    and wanting nowhere else to be—

Where I saw myself many years older—
    been around the world and back
    been to heaven—
        and back—
    and turned into the blessed sky above
    to wander with an angel—
    to live ten years in the mountains

        that always feel like home.

Maybe it was in the quiet serenity of a winter afternoon
    and the absolute simplicity
        of one man alone
        and the way it made me feel—

Like a Montana highway
    stretched out for miles

    no where to be
    no where to go—

    just simple—
    just content—

    just

    like

    that.

02.14.00 Streamwood

Some Things Take You Higher
poems from the journey home

A Long Time—A Letter To My Friend

Hello, again—
It's been a long time—

Yes, I'm living in Montana,
        it's a beautiful place—

Thirty minutes in my truck
        and you'd think you were on a different planet—
The Mission Mountains are just about the closest thing to Heaven
        I think I've ever seen—

Just North, near Flathead Lake,
        on the road to Glacier Nat'l Park,
        I go and sit, and look around
        and collect things
        to make these natural sculptures I've been working on—
            I build them on my porch,
            and now my porch is full—

They remind me of the different Native American burial markers—
        I have a lot of ideas for them—
        Sent two out so far—

You want one?—
        they're all different—
I'm going up again Saturday morning early—
        It's tough to put into words, but I did what I could
            in Mission Mountain Love Poem—

I spend most of the summer on the road again—
        after the Appalachian Trail,
        and extended stay in Georgia

Went back to Taos for a short time
        and down through southern New Mexico
        Sangre de Christos, too, are a little bit of satori—

        (I'll be there again—)

I met some really sweet girls walking down the street

        in Leadville, Colorado,
            wild, dreadlocked manes
            (made an appearance in
            Those Cosmic Companions—
            did you get that one?)

Went out to San Francisco and Berkeley–mad–chemists
        and stayed with Uncle Bob
            for two weeks or so waiting for him to finish his job
                so we could go out to High Sierra Music Festival
                in the Sierra Nevadas
                East San Francisco bay area
                bluegrass from the hills—

Spent the fourth of July with extended family in Longview, Washington
        on the Colombia River,
        Look across to the other bank—
            that's Oregon—

On our way to Mother Alaska!
        but stopped at the Canadian border just above Seattle—
        couldn't cross without paying two—hundred dollar fine—

Who knows—
        Young American Sadhus Need Not Apply

        turned around and jumped on Widespread Panic tour
            to Bozeman, Montana—

Jumped off and headed for Missoula—

Stayed one week in old hotel with Bob—
He bought some old beater of an auto for six hundred dollars
        from chain–smoking white man
        making a dollar in Montana

Leaked coolant and oil
        all the way back to Chicago
        (and broke down in Wyoming, nearly eaten by a bear)
            now he lives in Charleston, Illinois— *Chucktown*
            down by Eastern Illinois University
            going to school there—
            (car's dead)—

Changed hotels when bob left here—
>   Went to the Del Mar on Broadway
>   for another week looking for apartment—
>   Spent so much time dwelling on things those days,
>   hadda get out of the room and get a beer—
>   Saw this good looking bar one day out
>   looking at apartments
>   >   in town—
>   They have bands there, I thought—
>   That Friday I went,
>   >   only to get away for a while—
>   >   first night out here—

Met Darren, hammer—pounding carpenter from Squaw Valley,
>   85 miles north—
But then—
Then met this one chick who came up and talked to me,
>   she said she noticed my eyes—
>   I smiled them at her—

>   became my girlfriend for one month and a half—
>   Quite a surreal experience I gotta say
>   I felt I was living in some dream bubble the whole time
>   >   and I told her this
>   >   because I thought she would see
>   >   >   how much this meant to me—

Where did you come from? I asked her
>   in my arms for the first time

>   how do these things happen?

I wrote poetry about her for weeks
>   She was Montana to me
>   a mistake, I thought, in retrospect— But not really—

It's hard times now—
>   but then again, when isn't?
I need time to myself now
>   to be here, now
>   sit back and let it all sink in—
>   and I'm getting it—
>   Much, too much of it—

Town to town a million miles an hour—
        sometimes this is good—

Found Kailash Dharma Center and talked to John there
        Lives there and wants me to come to sunday teachings
            with Gen Kelsang Yangdzom
            to sit meditation there
            at the center mornings throughout the winter
            cold dark winter dawn when
            no one else is Awake
                they have a schedule set—
                this is good—

Tulku Sangak Rinpoche coming to Montana from Tibet
        (Nepal now since 1955)
        for teachings October 9–21 and November 9–14—
        Montana Buddhist Conference November 13—
        Makes me think of two Aspen monks,
            and our four day sessions—

I am applying to Naropa University—
Jack Kerouac School of Disembodied Poetics—
Allen Ginsberg and Ann Waldman founded 197—4?—

MFA in Poetics
        gotta send three letters of recommendation
        and fifteen pages of poetry—

Two year program with so much activity
        and great things going on there
        I would like to spend some time there
        study abroad in Nepal one semester,
            also, just sit—

Art Institute of Chicago wants me there—
So, if not Naropa then Chicago next year—

I don't want to be in the city right now though—

So, I'm just being here—

Saw Blues Traveler at the Warfield Theatre, S–F— with Uncle Bob
Saw Rat Dog and Widespread two nights in Aspen
with photographer Brent to talk to and the carbondale crew

Went two shows at the Gorge, Washington
Saw Widespread in Bozeman in old ice rink
Got in free to Ziggy Marley here in the park below my place

Fine Pickin's Bluegrass Festival on Marshall Mountain
       Bought a ticket tonight—

Leftover Salmon
Tony Furtado
Cold Mountain Rhythm Band

       told my boss today I hafta come in late the next day
       because we're sleeping out

       he said—   *Cool!*—

Hundreds of new poems
    the west is so good to me for that
    I will send you some periodically
        (book 5— this very being is It—
        book 6— Some Things Take You Higher—
        book 7— Purple Velvet Fictionpoems)

Sold three paintings here that shipped back to Chicago
    haddanother commission but the chick left town—

Lemme see some new fiction!
    Where's It At, and why you hidin' it?

John Popper Band touring East Coast
    Maybe *East Coast Rhythms?*—
    (shoulda went to Vermont afterall!
        first ever JPB show in Burlington)
Should be good—
    Most sincere songwriter we can see
        I love him for that—

I'll be back there Nov 19–28 for Thanksgiving
Maybe we can have a beer

        and talk about how far we've come this far—
Maybe I can get a look
        at that small miracle crawling around on your floor—
Irish temper and all—I would like that—

Good to hear from you, too— Forever and your friend—

PS Greasy Spoon Publishing has been modified—
        in awareness, been changed to Rhythm Mountain Studios,

        something that fit better, you see?

One of these days that will hang wooden carved on the outside of my gallery and studio somewhere in these crazy mountains—

        with a sign hanging below,
        blowing in the breeze that says this—
        Everyone Welcome.

o9.24.99 Missoula, MT

Clayton Delaney

Moonlit india ink
      midnight mountain highway

Substitute caffeine for sunlight
      french vanilla gas station cappuccino
      steaming up the windows
      and burning my tongue.

High speed fridged— late November air
      all the way to Colorado
      from Montana
      for Thanksgiving.

Where are you now, Mr. Po–lice–man?
      highway state patrol cars bottomed–out in the dust—
          rusting—
      into nothing

      feeding the worms, perhaps—
      something to look at on the side of the road,
      if I could see that far.

Black, cracked Sawtooth's on the horizon
      ghostly backlit by foggy spacestation moon

Idaho route twenty–eight
      the Salmon Highway
      and the Lost River Range

Waylon Jennings singing how he remembers the day
      Clayton Delaney died,
      the Original Outlaw howling loud
          in the midnight badlands

      of the West.

11.24.99 Salmon, ID
12.o3.99 Missoula, MT

I Met Edward Abbey Reincarnated As A Horse

I met Ed Abbey reincarnated as a horse,
> one day actually driving back to my friend's dry-rotted
> bats-in-the-attic
> A-frame house in the Roaring Fork Valley of Colorado.

I had spent the night in this house
> with several other people to celebrate a birthday.

I brought my birthday friend a copy of one of my books, this book,
> and in the loud, exciting confusion of reuniting long-
distance relationships—
> and beer—
> I forgot all about it, the book that is.
> And left it in the truck all night.

So in the early mountain morning fog
> after I left once,
> I remembered the book and drove back to the old A-frame,
> and that's when I met Edward Abbey,
> > reincarnated as a horse.

I knew it was Ed right off because of the long-legged high hip cowboy swagger in his step.

I knew it was Ed right off because his white beard shone the years lazily on his chin.

I knew it was Ed because the worn patches on his knees
> and sunburn on his nose
> > from so much time spent kicking around in the desert
> > > —alone,
> > > or in the canyonlands of Utah.

I knew it was Ed because he stood dusty and firm
> in the sage brush and cactus on the land.

I knew it was Ed because I could see it in his eyes
> as he stared at me
> and I stared at him
> and stood with the mountains to my back,
> > the indian summer snow-capped peaks reflected in his eyes

No more than a days walk away
    —that's how Ed likes it,

    always has,
    always will.

11.27.99 Emma, CO

Absolute Liberation

Don't need this job for the money,
        but the involvement is nice.
Don't need these hours kept daily,
        but my schedule is right.
Don't need no friends in this foreign town
        to break my heart and call me back
        when they feel they're ready,
        but the affection felt good.

Don't need a girl I thought was Love
        that vanished around the block
Don't need shoes— but I like the ones I have
        to run miles in the grass
        or stand barefoot in the sand

Don't need a thing.
        Just want my truck—
        a removed part of me
                seventy–seven thousand miles across the map
                you keep it on you're bookshelf,

        well, I've been there.

        So far, forty–eight states,
            Canada and Mexico,
            and much further to go—

Just want my music
        and some hot chocolate in the evenings
        with my books.

Don't need this town—
        gossip town—
        pack up my things (—books, poems, and paintings)
            to maybe never come back.

Don't need another education that takes years to get,
        but then again, yes, I do.

        we'll make this a list, I say,

             to go along with the rest—

I need that music
          and I love my friends
I need my books,
          and I got my pens
          and poems
          and paintings to keep me Here.
I'll keep my truck, because it takes me there.

But what I don't need,
          what I really can do without
          all the menial happenings over which
                    I have no control.

          All the madness that comes with these emotions—
          the laconic head dress that seems to come along
          with the rest.

          But, then again—

          yes, I do.

o9.15.99 Montana

Eventual List Poem

I have some new things to do eventually,
        and eventually they will get done.

I have to get those canvases stretched,
        perfect with effort—
        and eventually they will get primed
        and painted—
        hang on the wall of Chicago, Denver or NYC.

I have to send in more poems— juried shows across the country,
        and eventually they will get sent—
        printed black on stark white paper
            and published.

I have to find John Popper lyrics to satisfy my curiosity,
        and eventually read
        and keep close to my heart.

I have to sew handmade patch of Ganesh from Nepal to my pack,
        and eventually it will be secure
        and go with me everywhere.

        Shine in the sun.

I have to call Kara in post–Europe homeless un–confusion near Dallas,
        and eventually we will laugh
        and wonder when we'll see each other again.

I have to find cardboard boxes,
        suitable for shipping hand made sculptures
        and wrap them secure
        for southern California and Carbondale, Colorado—

I have to do laundry, that never was mine,
        only borrowed from thrift stores across the country,
        but the clothes stink in my room,
        so now they need washed.

I have to find out about Washington state shows at the Gorge,
        and eventually I will go,
        but I need the information

        then sit solemn in the sun.

I have to get that wooden smiling Buddha statue from Berkeley,
        and eventually it will sit in my room,
        but how do I get it, and where is it now?—

I have to find east Indian Allen Ginsberg pajamas,
        for Ramayana Samsara
        everyday cycle classic Hindu epic dance
        and eventually I will—

        or maybe I won't—

        just sit tall manjursri in the mountains of western America
                orderly Bodhisattva,
                keeping my lists,

                one by one—
                and taking care of it all—

o9.15.99 Montana

Montana Meditation Sounds

Some days I sit meditation in a small room—
    empty white walls
    off the kitchen.
    Do you know my kitchen?—

Some mornings I sit meditation in my room—
    so quiet I can hear the river,
    two blocks away—
    Ever see that river?—

Some nights, right back in the same spot,
    sitting straight
    flat spine rising to the ceiling,
    I wish there was no ceiling at all.

        Legs crossed calmly— barefoot silence
            in my room.

        Thoughts come in,
            and float away like bubbles in a stream—
    Watch each breath come in and out,
    and disappear into nothingness in front of my face.

Silence now but for that humming rattle
    of the refrigerator from nineteen seventy—two
    constant trickle out the frozen pipes in back.
        And then it's gone.

Pacific Northwest freight train whistle
        out the window
            far off in the distant night blackness—
Dirty hobos, and fresh dug coal from the mountains.
Somewhere out there.
        And then it's gone.

I hear wild, young skateboard kids
    pass by down below
    grinding wheels on cement
    Where you off to?—
        And then they're gone.

I hear young woman across the street—
        wooden yellow lit front room in the window
        framed by forty foot maple trees,
        playing grand piano Gershwin or Beethoven
                like Frank O'Hara in NYC,
                      or Grafton, Massachusetts
                      nineteen forty–two——

                And then it's gone.

I hear dogs barking far off and quiet
        wanting food
        or company
        or just that old tattered beat up tennis ball
                turned yellow with age——

                And then they're gone.

I hear myself, ten years old in Illinois
        yelling and running in the street—
        scabbed knees
        sunburnt face sweating in August sun
                summer vacation in full swing—

                Then— like bubbles in a stream——

                I'm gone.

09.13.99 Missoula, MT

Coffee Shop Mantra

And through the squeaky wooden door
    of the coffee shop
    came a giant of a man, and ancient
    with a wild, grey, log cabin beard
    that vibrated when he smiled,
    and the kindest voice I've heard
    in a long, long time...

"Well, does he look sleepy?.."
    he asked his wife, maybe,
    referring to Jack, their ten-year-old Newfoundland
        who had parked himself quite contentedly
        out front waiting patiently
        near the cedar benches
        and wooden saddle-horse sculpture,
            among the paying early morning customers

    and their crumbs.

In his hands the old man carried two brown-recycled paper cups of coffee,
    steaming hot in the cold morning air
    that felt so new,
    and fresh in my lungs.

Jack, I thought, great name...
    and trotted off.

I don't know for sure if this man, his wife and his dog even exist
    but I like to think they do.

    And now I'm sure of it,
    Six days later and it's nearly ten o'clock...

On my street,
    mammoth beast four-wheel-drive
    highway locomotive
    pulls in for fresh coffee
    or fancy french frilly baked pastry

engine running,
        no one inside.

He's rich, say, gotta big car.

        Goest, though, capitalist America,
            shining in the night

        Gold coins in your pockets,

        But the bright stars over my head
        Eternal Gold Heart,
            the Mission Mountains of the west,
            and the smell of autumn fading into winter—

        worth more that all those coins

            and on a scale so grand
            even those hungry pockets of yours
            could never understand.

I can see my breath now
        cold winter night
        under these stars.

And see that girl
        sitting quiet through the glass
        front window of old wooden coffee shop bakery
            on the street where I walk

See that girl smiling now at me through the glass
        out to the street.
            I smile back and she looks back.

Gunna find that girl
        or let her find me.
        Sit there warm
            maybe share a secret
            that she doesn't know is a secret

Maybe tell her a story from the road,
        of gangland needless violence in Memphis—
            no, no violence

           of golden prose meditation on the edge of Big Sur—
                   no, no religion,
        of the Sangre de Christo's, and Arroyo Hondo,
                northern New Mexico Mountains on my mind.

Maybe read her a poem,
        and pay a dollar for her tea.

        Honey or milk with that tea?

Would you see me again
        and remember my name
        like you did to my surprise just a few days before.

Tell me your dreams, maybe I'll tell you mine.
Maybe I'm in your dreams, maybe you're in mine,
        from time to time.

Walking mindful on my street
        cold Rocky Mountain winter air
        creeping down my neck,
        on my way for hot coffee
                any time of day,
                any day,
                but Saturday's the best, you see,

                that much, I say,
                I know for sure.

10.17.99 Missoula

Idaho

I spent the day at the hot springs,
    where did they go?..
    Raced to Idaho
    wrote poems along the way.

I spent the day in naked warm water,
    and no one cared.
    But you, and you were naked too;
    and your smile.

I spent the day thinking,
    the way I always do.

        Red-green alpine forest with steam
            afternoon sunshine orange light,
            sat still on a rock,
            river's edge icy cold.
        And warm inside for hours.

I spent the day with vagabond stranger,
    walking barefoot on those rocks
    bearded and blond
    asking to sit in...
    and made good talk.

I spent the day contemplating old theories,
    with mexican-american
        grandmother's child of the southwest.
    Talked about this perfect place,
        evolution,
        and religion in the American Midwest Classroom.

I spent the day watching Mother Nature's creatures,
    widespun pollen yellow jacket bees,
    ultraviolet blue-hazel dragonflys
    spinning and hovering over my head...
    A mother moose,
        full grown to size
        caring and drinking cold river
        with one-year-old child.

Get ready for winter, I say,

    the snow's coming fast,
    six thousand feet dusted with powder

    under the trees
    and it's not even fall—

Stopped on the road
    traded for topaz,
    from Utah and New Mexico.
    Broken, hand cracked rock.
    Old man highway in his van.

Where will you be come winter?

I'll be with the mountains,
    harsh snowfall feeding grounds for mother moose and her child—
      Rocky Mountain sun in the arms
        of Idaho.

08.31.99 Montana

this very being is It.

West Coast Rhythms

There is a place I once heard of
called Instamatic Playground Freeze——
    a gone, tall site
    ragged and torn around the edges,
    and satori sunlight sky——
        Inside.

Where city streets, dark and lonely old
    turn to plush velvet curtains
    and porcelain white toilet seats,
    shag carpet from the nineteen—forties
        stained and spotted by imported beer
        at two bucks a pint
        and cherry cigarette holes
            black,
            and crispy around the edges——

Decorate!
    and make holy——

    bronze statues of Oedipus,
        Phaedrus
        and Goliath

            detail scratch proof surface
            tarnished around the edges
            make good company
                for those who came alone
                and are here
                only for the band

Where *Slaughterhouse Five,*
    Franny and Zoey
    Far Off Places,
    and *Turtle Island*
    ornamate the dusty shelves
        of red tarnished oak
        and maple leaf hardwood
        bronze belly buddha corners
        and a smile that makes me feel at home
        and brings me home,

                spinning cotton, hand–sewn skirts
                opening set two
                on a taffy apple hardwood discotec floor
                in beat town San Francisco,
                the bridges on the Bay
                and one paisley barefoot angel
                to Monterey
                or Big Sur
                and all the naked beaches in between

Where the sunny ocean tide–blown rock
        after full–day composition campfire madmen
        take time to run to the cabin
        or general store
        of barefoot wine and rain puddles
        gathered in misty haven of Pacific downpour
                and Redwoods,
                just to dance in sunset satori
                in broken harbor midnight dreams
                and the moon that won't quit

Or Jesus–built highways sing humming songs
        in your ear for doing nothing
        but flinch–not, my friend,
        for death is on this road
        deep curves and radio–active
                campers on the bend
                will haunt you
                or wake you
                from mid–day zazen
                or zafu–pillow meditation in the sand——

And where, then will you be,
        but right back in that Portland town,
        metal–can bonfires on the edge of town—
                newspapers,
                and cardboard—

                pink panther insulation
                blowing wild in the streets

                the velvet homeless,
                black and white and gold—
                and the Portland Theatre—
                blinking and glowing straight through

                    from dusk till dawn—

            coffee bean renaissance heaven
                    sit softly, now,
                    and don't say a word

For these are the Rhythms of the West——
            beating fast in my heart
            pounding loud on the pavement or sending ripples
deep and holy, or wicked all the same through the long hot sands of the
Coastland beaches and sunproof sugar umbrellas,
            spotted in the surf.

Oh— Big Sur— you did for me what no one else could—
        magic carpet west coast rocks battered by ultraviolet waves—

        You showed me the truth
                        —it's all *Inside*,
        and forgiveness—
                Right Mindfulness, and Right Concentration and to
                        never stop asking why

                to these questions that come to me in the night, half
asleep—or half Awake on my wine stained porch
                in the snowy Montana mountains—
                        Bitterroot Range,
                high above the sea and the west coast beaches—
                pounding rhythmic beats
                        sand turtles
                        and starfish

            where I sat naked, dirty
                    long hair, alone
                    calm inside——
                    and golden in the sun——

                    Manjursri bodhisattva,
                        where *this very being is It*.

08.03.99 Missoula, MT

Rocky Mountain Sidewalk Sutra

This is the endless learning
        crackhouse of evolution
        and mystic doorway possibilities—
        coffee and speed caffeine in the street
        mad bicycles on the mountain horizon
                hanging christmas lights on my wooden porch
                to the sound of the three piece band on the corner

sturdy bookshelf from the alley
        broken toilets
        no money
        meditation future freedom liberation
        beautiful blond girls on green bikes
                or on foot
                but mostly on bikes

    writing poetry and prosody
            and painting in my head

    pamphlet flyer free–wind pages
on Mumia–Abui Jamal
        self defense or murder?—
        freedom or prisoner?

    late night jazz bands
        in smokey portal bars
        on Front Street by the river

Weirdo visitors weird on me—
        think me weird—
        and *"do you believe in God?"*
                that old man in the sky?——
                white bearded patrol gate operator
                let me in,
                let me in—

        is that your god?
        gold–lame dresses
                and diamond cloud sandals.

        (No, no god here—
        god is in here, god is out there and inside of me)

I'll start my own Rocky Mountain Mahayana tradition
    diamond vehicle Vajra rituals

        are no rituals
        no conceptions
        no limits

India Ink paintings
    of cowboys and indians
    in the gallery windows
    signed with my mountain peak moons
    dated for eternity

Passers by say nothing—
    just stare bug–eyed and frozen—

Decorate your home! I say—
    hang up your passions—
    take a good look

    a twisting birthday pinata
    full of gold–chocolate possibilities
    back when you were nine—

Where are you now, two–wheeled angel—
    come back again
    and again——
    every night by the river
        and I'll re–invent the midnight sky—
        moonlight constellations
            with new stars in it.

07.22.99 Missoula, MT

Afternoon Sunset America

I've seen desert mornings and had a bit of heaven——

I've sold painting for thousands of dollars in Chicago galleries
and in the West—

I've driven coast to coast USA, and everywhere in between—

I've fallen in love with the most perfect person in the world—

I've played in the snow—
        and walked twenty-six miles over Schofield Pass,
           Colorado
        from Marble to Crested Butte—
        pack on my back—
        with my dog, the single most wonderful friend
        I could ever have—

I've seen fireworks fourth of July Soldier Field
        after *his* last show,
        and sat dumfounded and amazed
        with my friends in the night—

I've given a poem, and made cry with happiness
        and contentment—
        and have written two hundred more

I've sat in October New Mexico Sangre de Christo Mountains
        handmade sweater on my back—
        Holy Southwestern sun on my face
        and thought of the future—

I've roamed naked in the hot springs of Idaho
        with my friends from Montana
        and made hot chocolate campfire
        in the sunset forests—

I've laughed so hard I can't breath—
        tears come streaming down my face—

            and I've laughed again thinking back on it

I've slept 400 nights in my truck
    no job
    no money
    no friend—
    just my thoughts in the forest—
        or lonely faraway mountains—
            or truck stop Texarkana South—

I've built sculptures with Mother Natures remains
    from Flathead Lake, Montana
    and sent them across the country in the mail—

I've lived eight months in Rocky Mountain log cabin
    early january mountain morning frost
    and every morning want to go back—

I've been broken hearted more than once
    I've been broken hearted now,
    and had the Mission Mountains to make me smile—

    and I'll always have that—

And now I've seen Holy Washington sun set slow—
    yellow–blues over pink–dusted clouds—
    orange and warm—
    hanging low touching my face—

    deep green grass whispering in the breeze
        of late afternoon west
    and reaching down to sandstone ampitheatres
    where I've found a little bit of Heaven———

    once again—
    in America.

09.15.99 Missoula, MT

I wanted to write this poem about all the brothers and sisters I've met over the past seven years of traveling the roads of America (going back to Woodstock and the east coast trip of 1994). I don't really consider myself on the road all the way back to 1994, but I did take this extended trip in August of that year. I did meet some great people—one or two that really stick out. Really, though, I think the trip with Robbie Miller in the fall and winter of 1996 started the idler way of life. So, from there is where I consider the start of my life on the road.

This poem describes some of the amazing lunatics, generous folks, Zen wanderers and down–to–earth kindness I've met along the way. I call it *Those Cosmic Companions*. This is a dedication of sorts and those who it is dedicated to may or may not know, but they are the people, the brothers and sisters of this life, *the road*, and who will stay with me forever.

Those Cosmic Companions

New age karma
        American Dharma——
Red hot hazy morning
        roadside sunrise.

Hundreds of small time
US towns and cities
        and all the mountains
        north of Mexico.

And New Mexico is the
        place I met some of these cosmic companions of the road—

        New Age Kings
                of purple majestic two lane highways——

Where George in Taos who borrowed
        my knife for free–red opium
        mystic harvest possibilities—
        but got none because too many people know—

          and talked for hours
          in Kit Carson park
          about adobe homes
          and subterranean domes
              of privacy
              in the raw American desert.

Where JF in Rocky Mountain
      two month haze
      and homesickness—
      The Allman Brothers setting sun in western Colorado
ultraviolet Red Rock night—
          I left for two months
          and you called me back
          to snowy Vermont
          in daily graveyard walks
          with the dogs
              through the Green Mountains
              pool–hall smokey room
              gangland heaven
          and the grandest parking lot snowball fight
              of all time
          Where I came– to stay—
              till our time ran out——

Where in Leadville Colorado—
      three beautiful and natural
      handmade dresses
      and eyes of azure that matched the sky—
          a crimson mane,
          wild and dreadlocked
          in the barefoot mountaintop wind—
              asked me for a walk—
              gotta drive on,
              I smiled—
              but I'll see you in Taos
              and Santa Fe
              and we'll walk together——
              Then——

Where JT the simplest of them all
      and the one I loved the most.
      Farm–raised from Indiana

>   I saw you two years running
>   morphine sunrises
>   in two–bit campgrounds
>   in the heartland.
>   We talked until dawn
>   and laughed out loud at menial jobs
>   and the naivete of it all—
>   we'd never live nine to five
>   and we knew it then.
>   We live it now.
>
> Where'd you go my brother?——
> What shows got you back on the road?—
>   back in your soft top jeep
>   breaking and entering
>   in long–winded blues harp
>   Lysergic Diethylamide nights
>   the headlights and a parking lot
>   the size of Mars——
>
>   Or is that where we went?——
>
>
> Where the fastest–man–alive
>   borrowed mountain bikes and rode all night
>   in broken bone
>   twisted–spoke hysterics
>   and talked from the Peoria River to the
>   mad bars of Main Street
>   and River City jazz clubs
>   that ruled the night
>   for hours
>   at high–speed ecstasy
>   moonlight phantasm—
>   the girls that treated us like movie stars
>   and clung on booze soaked
>   matchstick rooftops
>   and howled at the moon——
> The madness of turning
>   over your own car
>   for kicks and leaving it
>   for the rats, the dandelion weeds,
>   and police man brutality
>   in the alleyways of Peoria——
> Mad hipster with cosmic vibrations—

                Barcelona circus freak
                where have you gone, Goofy?—
                I'll see you again.

Where freaked–out wanderers
        came in hitchhiked,
        cold and hurt
        to hot coffee in Suches, Georgia—
        where Britt runs this place
        for two wheeler motorcycle dulcimer gangsters
                of the lazy south

You didn't help us, I told her—
        You saved us—
        Warn out and beat—
        afraid of the tornado we just walked through
        like the marathon monks
                of India and the Himalayas
                no where to go
                but on
                and we did—
And *please, please me* Haley Murphy—
        in your destined sidewalk
        Southern California greetings
        you wrapped hemp in my long tangled hair——
we ate tacos
                and drank budweiser
                and talked about Malibu—
                we'd surf come morning—
                New Years Eve in Chicago
                        glowing blue electric pants
                        the ancient magic dragon
                you hung around my neck
                      still tells me the story
                      and reminds me of you
                      and our trip
                      and how it came
                      to a drastic end———

Halo nights in the distant Southwest—
        Las Vegas casinos
        in thrift store suits
                non fishing bee sting remedy strangers

                        in Mississippi ten days
                        in Arizona—
                        Carbondale Rainbow family gathering
                        lazy day Monopoly
                        Eagle Nest New Mexico
                        Discotec Hollywood
                        the Sunset Strip
                        Girls from Australia tagged along from Nevada
                                in satin electric jackets
                                bounce and spin till dawn—
Where are you now—
            in cocaine Chicago
            Wicker Park nights
            our oil paint floor
                        of Winchester Street——

Tigers
and pandas
and grizzly bears
on cheap canvas
            for hundreds of dollars
            in small Damen Avenue galleries—
Bob Dylan turntable blues
Creedence the malamute
            defecating in rat–infested
            trash can alleys.
North Damen Milwaukee nights
            and Liquid Soul at Double Door
            arrested in Effingham
            back in the city
            Unseasonably cool
            Robbie Robbie with your Duane Allman antics,
                    and high–speed brown van tantics—

            —a heart of gold
        when you have it————

And all you *freaks*
        bums
        gadabouts
        sweethearts
        drag queens
        junkies
        angels

    feens
    tea–heads
    drunks
    rock stars
    NO–*bodies*—
    chaps, bloaks,
    generous strangers
    Zen wanderers
    down–to–earth kindness
    absolute hysterics
    brothers and sisters of America
       and Australia
       and England
       and Asia—

Everyone and everything—
    the Dharma of the road

    and where it took me—
    and where you took me—

And so here we are one more day
    or one more show
    let it play
    and let it go——

Because there are no Buddhas
    no mystics
    no conceptions
    no directions—
    Only Right Mindfulness——

    just what you see
       laid out in front of you—
    just what you find inside of you
       or on the road
    and then in your mind—

    vajrayana lotus diamond——

      Bodhisattva wanderers
      Pratyekabudda manjursri—

those cosmic companions—

on my endless——peaceful
American road.

06.17.99 Big Sur, CA (for Mark McPhillips)

Don't Want To

Don't want to be immaculate and rich
Don't want to drink diamonds after morning tea
Don't want to spell my name in octopus ink
Don't want to eat dinner with the president's wife
    or play hide and seek with her kids
    or make speeches to her kids' friends

Don't want an IV in my arm
    in hospital pajamas, weak,
    lonely, and watching bad T.V—

Don't wanna be hassled by junk mail,
    or turn away fan mail—
    everyone gets fan mail
Don't wanna pay the cable guy
Don't want to be the cable guy
Don't want to wait in line
    for groceries
    or used Levi's
    or a brand new strawberry–banana daiquiri
    blenders from the store

Don't wanta haffta have
    money in my pocket
Don't wanta remote control
Don't want tax returns in the spring
Don't want taxes on my beer
Don't want taxes on my lettuce
    or tomatoes
    and organic fatless milk in my fridge

Don't want viral spinal meningitis
    or the headaches
    or a spinal tap to make sure
Don't want a phone bill
    because I don't want a phone
Don't want chemicals in my kitchen
    or a pay stub every friday
    or every other friday—
    mostly, though,
    don't want a boss that gives me that pay stub
Don't want charcoal–mining dust in my lungs

>   or any dust at all for that matter
> Don't want gold frame pictures on my wall
>
> Don't want to pick up that lucky penny in the sand
>   or a cover charge to see my band
> Don't want to sit in traffic
> Don't want wrong–minded–missing–brain–neighbors
>   or a landlord that doesn't care.
>
> Don't want AIDS
>   or a deficient system inside
>   that can't tell right from wrong.
>
> Don't want strangers
>
>   or anything that takes me from where I want to be
>
>   from my long–haired American sadhus
>   on the streets where I live
>
>   from Gyalwa Karmapa—
>   Kagyu sect of Tibetan Buddhism
>   and Dainin Katagiri Roshi—
>   purple vairochana earthly saint
>   on cold Saturday afternoons,
>   but Always in my heart,
>   and Always on my mind—
>
>   from Ramayana,
>   classic Hindu epic dance, and
>   from the brightly colored satin bodices
>   and twisting lengths of silk
>
>   from my room where you can sit
>   and get high by osmosis,
>   contemplating the infinite complexity
>   of the human imagination—
>
>   from manjursri bodhisattva, completely
>   and infinitely of wisdom and learning—
>
>   from Allen, the king of Majalis,
>   bearded white–gown Indian pajamas
>   in Moscow and Prague—
>   kicked out socialist republics—

wrapped in red drapes
        and cardboard crown–septor jewels
        playing hand cymbals to
        beat down
        down town
        or shanty–town

        Hare Om Namo Shiva
        and Om Sri Maitreya
        fully costumed from 1890,
        the Kral Majalis
        May King of Czechoslovakia and Cuba—
        but mostly just You, A.G.,
            and N.C.
        and the greatest minds of the Lower East Side
        or San Francisco
            ranting and *Howl*—ing
            on the Free–est soil on Earth—

        —America.

from this newly–wed evolution
        Meditation Generation—

        Pratyekabuddha,
        self made mystics in the streets—
        it's not where you're going,
        but how you're getting there—

from my wooden studio easel
        handmade in New Mexico
        oil paint stained,
        where I keep my heart
        and create even more—

from the wind horse candle light prayer flags
        ornamenting my porch
        or statue of Ganesh—
        Elephant God of India
        in the lightening storms
        of the late summer Rocky Mountain West

from Bodhiccita, altruistic mind of enlightenment,

        the Aspen monks,
        and Right mindfulness is the only way

from my spider weed couch
    found in the alley
    covered with Mexican blankets
    and cardboard boxes shipped from home—

Sit comfortably again, tonight
    and fall asleep again, tonight

    one
    more
    time.

o8.o5.99 Montana

Haiku 12

A muse flashes in my head
as I sit in the sun
      I call it Sun Dried Tomato.

Sun Dried Tomato

We gotta find summer——
              Summer?—
   Yeah.
              But we're in it——
*Not **in** it—*
Find it——

Find it over red rock arches lit by the sun—
       Craggy rocks broken by the water
             and clouds
                  and wind
                       of the Colorado Plateau—

Find it in Big Sky Country
       where clouds don't exist
       and maybe never will—
Where old bums sit on the bank
       of Lake McDonald
       and talk of ex–wives on the edge—
Where going to the sun road
       creaks and curves on skinny–one–lane byways
       with RV's at nine thousand feet—

Find it in early morning September campfire
       and the sunrise of Glacier National Park
       and her mountains—

And find it sitting there— Alone—

Find it at Saint Mary's— eighteen miles south of Canada
       and Waterton

        and Alpine Peaks you won't believe with your own eyes—

Find it in Nevada
        on hot open road that stretches
        and goes

        and goes——

In the sunset headed west
        that never ends
        but just hangs there reminding you—

                of what?——

                      just reminding you—

Find it at Jackson Wyoming
        before you arrive
        twenty miles south of town
        where coyotes and wolves in the black mountainside
                cry you to sleep—

Where the Tetons, snowcapped and amazed
        created the fortress of medieval cowboys
        and broken wheel wagons—
        where the moon washes over
                and another river roars along–side my truck—
                      at least for today——

Find it Southwest in New Mexico
        where it's been for years
        in the banks of the Rio Grande
                and the trails and dried wood of the
                Sangre de Christos
                      east of Taos—
                      the most magical place of them all—

And in the naked women from San Francisco
        in the hot springs of Arroyo Hondo
        twenty miles north of town
                north of the Sacred Circle
                north of Eagle Nest
                      with my dog

              and Wheeler Peak distant now
              in the Red River Valley—

Find it on the coast
      of foamy white beach madness
      and rainy dried warped wood

      of Kesey's place in La Honda
          through morning mist
          and a nap in the sand—

Find it in the stars so bright it makes you laugh
      and in the moonlight reflecting back off midnight snow
          in Redstone, Colorado—
          a broken heater
          and cabin #14—

Find it too— in the sacred splendor
      of cosmic companions digging the open road—

And pack up late night for Lavender Canyon
      fourteen miles off road
      over red rock and cactus—
          Abbey country—
      The Needles entrance to the Canyonlands
          where we dreamed awake
          on mushrooms handed down
          by the Yuma Indians
          of another century—
              hand blown rock art
              and a sign to say they survived———
              vajra lotus diamond vision—

And look in the Redwoods—
      northern California
      Oregon monsters
      that will cradle you
          and sing you a song as you sleep—

And in the cabins up there

early dawn mist and a soggy sleeping bag
        inside warm orange lit huts
        set firm on the beaches
        and rock dropped slippery dew

    of my Pacific Northwest—

Find it in the sun
        of lazy Texarkana truck stops
        and gas stops along broken freeways
        and beer can alleys of the South—

Where Marlboro signs nailed to the wall
        still hang from 1950
        with glass bottle Coca–Cola coolers in the shade—

        But mostly— mostly you'll find it right there—
    Right there in front of where you stand
        or sit behind the wheel
        ornamenting this world with your sincerity—

        crazy wind at seventy miles—

        What is your name?——

        Sun Dried Tomato,

        and she smiled.

04.25.99 Streamwood, IL

Barefoot Mountain

Ancient dusty pink
    adobe churches
    one room
    new-found freedom
    in sandalwood twin-twisted crucifix
        cracked and buried in the sand.

Arroyo Seco in
    Holy Trina Magna
    hot seat
    cold feet
    azure midnight sky.

The quiet desert midday sun
    warms me
    watches me
    and reminds me I am home.

Black moon in Santa fe.

Santa Fe has that sky
    that sky that never ends.
    And the mountains
        stillness on the horizon
        that just sit
        just sit and let themselves be seen.

        Just sit.
        right here.
        right now.

Barefoot lotus mountains
    Zoto zen posture
    sitting high in
        purple rocky mountain
        zafu pillow heaven.

06.06.99 Quemado, NM

Why I Walk

A certain *one—ness* in this question
        a certain wholeness easily answered
        when that first step is taken

        heavy weight on my back
        provisions of mine
        weighing down my pack
                off into the unknown—
                that certain uncertainty
                of sandy hills
                or mountains
                or brotherhood of loony hysterics
                that carries me
                and pushes me
    to the further unknown—
                because it is there.

I find myself walking
        walking there
        walking because it is there
        walking because Wolf Den Gap
                in Suches, Georgia
                is a fine place to stay
                and be warm for a night
                safe and fed
                        hot coffee
                        and hot cocoa
                        and a banana
                along side half pound burgers
                and my brother
                        laughing hysterically in
                        Nowhere's–ville Dulcimer South
                        where Britt and the two wheeled riders
                        from Mississippi
                        make us feel welcome
                              make us feel at home
                              and safe
                              and so we stay
                              to dry out tornado soaked
                              hail beaten gear
                      and boots that squish when we walk—

I walk because Jim Hendrix
    in Appalachian Memories
    and Steel String Hymns
        makes me feel at home at T.W.O.
            toothbrush heaven
            because it's warm and dry
    and six string
    white bearded acoustic man
    feels at home here
        and so do we
        in the late–night storm whipped south
            of Georgia.
    where four day heavy nonstop rains
    turned to hail
    and a tornado laughing
        from two counties East
            brings us here—
            brings us home
            and safely back to sanity.

I walk to see the Black Mountain Pottery
    in bumpy Appalachia
    endless rainbow trout
    whistling and jumping
    into hitchhiked pickup truck
    wastelands of the North Georgia Mountains

Where "hope I was a little help"
    is frequently heard
    from wonderful right minded
        mystic old men
        on their way to wherever
    And Blood Mountain rages
        and burns up to 4800 feet above
        the sweet sea level way down below.

I walk for Even Stephen
    seventy eight years old
    the trail angel
    who hands out free mountain dews
    because you look like you could use a free pop—

    two mints to get you up
        Hogpen Gap—
    the steepest of them all

        and Hogpen Springs—

we checked em out
with handmade benches
made of trees and sweat
and maybe lonely afternoons to fill your time.

But here you are
and we love you, Even Stephen
        in every sense of the word
        because we don't know you
        but now we know you
        sunburnt and happy
        in your mountain home
                of the northern Georgia
                Appalachian Trail.

I walk because Terry Fox from Canada
        and Steve Prefontaine from Oregon
        never stopped.

I walk because utter confusion
        turns to bubbles of a stream
        and floats away—
        and clears my head.

I walk because time
        patience
                and nature
                        are the three great physicians.

I walk because it makes Cassidy smile.

I walk for Cactus Ed Abbey
        and the endless canyonlands
        of the magic southwest
                the javalinas
                the catalpa trees
                the acacia beans
        and the wind—soaked hard rock
        sandy spur medicine men
                of my American S.W—

I walk because Alex did.

I walk because Nando Luis—
>agave–flower stalk poolman of Atlanta
>waves hello on day four
>and gives me the thumbs up

I walk for the long haired white sadhus
>of Rocky Mountain America
Marble Canyon lost souls
>over Schofield Pass—
>brown bear capital of the west
>unknown to me
>and high powered vision camouflage men
>with your ATV and rifle
>have no place here

I see myself there alone,
>hazy morning
>five miles long at eleven thousand feet
>sunrise magic that brings tears to my eyes

And I walk for the disabled who cannot.

I walk for Lana, Laura, and Julia
>of Leadville, Colorado
>in wild mountain Americorp dresses
>handmade and golden
>who try to be here— but are not.

I walk for the culture rich
Bolivian musicians deep in southern California
>Mexico border sun
>playing hard from the Andes—
>ride flute, wind—harp madness in El Cajon
>and the summer desert air

I walk for my brother
        in mole skin antiseptic
        quaker–size blisters
        who keeps me going—
        even from two thousand miles away.
A stress fracture not on my foot
        but in my head
        that creaks and cracks
        with every step of this rocky endless
        Appalachian Trail

For the early morning Big Sur cliffs
        cracked and beaten by wind
        and waves
        and the sun that has not yet risen

I hear you loud, crazy dogs of the California coastline
        I hear you now and
        when morning comes
        I hear you again—

so come home at last
        on your howling moonlight run—
        down to the beaches crashing wild a hundred feet below—
        come back home and I'll call it even

                and fall asleep content,
                one   more   time.

06.17.99 Big Sur, CA (for Cassidy)

Princess Suede Black

I think I fall in love
        all too easily—
I think I fell in love
        at the swimming pool

        four hundred degree day
        locked in boiling
            automobile
            sun screen lotion
            burning my skin

        shady, cool water
            three feet
            four feet
            or six feet deep
                no diving allowed

Iced tea dripping down my chin
        I saw a pale young princess—
            too young for royalty
            bouncing and carrying on
            with her four year old
            sinking brother boy

I see you but you can't see me
                      see you
        so I watch you
        over Ginsberg biography
            paper back
            broken in
            road dust and torn
            is my privacy

I see you look at me
        wondering maybe,
        or concentrating on the kid

You looked again
        from three feet—
        water level at your hips
        arms above your head

        twirling hair over that wonderfully evil
            glistening body

        beautifully pale
        and curved
        at all the right times–

        baby smooth skin
            up to your shining breasts
            thinly clad in wet black bikini top

How old are you? and would you
        come home with me?—

        wash in the tub
        and I'll read you comics
        and poetry
            of Rousseau
            and angel–Blake
            and everything you wouldn't understand

        I have no home
        no home to take you to
            then maybe I would
            and we could lay together
                wet bathing suits soaking the carpet
                at the foot of the bed

And then I'll leave
        maybe visit you, or marry you, or maybe never come back
        to ask once again for the key to unlock the gate of this
        swimming pool under the sun.

        dripping wet,
        baby smooth skin, exotic belly dancer from the west

            and your princess
            suede
                    black
                          bikini

            that drives me mad.

06.30.99 San Francisco

Apartment Poem

Sitting at this olden beat kitchen,
    featured Saturday Evening Post
    Norman Rockwell in 1953

    with a noisy draining refrigerator
        and the window out onto the wooden porch—
        candlelight prayer flags overlooking
            my crooked–paved
            two way dead end street below

this table and chair set was top of the line fashion
        when Senator McCarthy was at the top of his game
        but now it creaks
            from side to side
            during honey wheat pancake breakfasts
            and black coffee–ring stains for two

refried beans and ten pound
brown rice bags on the shelf

Dirty potatoes on the counter top

Beautiful purple vairochana flowers
    in long–emptied beer bottles

        and Gary Snyder on the cupboard
            black and white
            solemn in Japan
            nineteen sixty–three.

o7.25.99 Missoula

A Day in the Life

An entire generation
        of new, young American sadhus—
        all following a path,
        and I think of you.

Through gentle poverty
    resonating marijuana glass
        parking lots
        and city streets
        or mountain trails

Coast to coast
        Right Minded highway ramblers
        up north to Alaska,
        and didn't we meet in Tijuana
        last time around?..

    tea drinking binges
        on the Colombia River bank

        Denver or Dharammsala?

        bring your blankets
        for a good nights sleep,
        nag champa in my bag—
            gives me away—
            or that's what I'll be—

                a gift to the wind
                and clouds
                and open road sunny day
                Rocky Mountain horizon.

Rejoice! I say
        we're all alive and well
        looking for love,
            and kicks—
            free coffee of green tea for a dime

Wood flute sidewalk show
        hopscotch girls
        in handmade dresses
        screaming wildly
                and naked in the river under the moon.

"Where is the center?—"
        the center of what?
        Osel Shen Phen Ling,
        the Mahayana center here in town—

        Diamond vehicle white cotton bodies,
        tan and firm

        from a diet of rice
                and beans,
                soy nuts and coffee

                or chick peas and stale pita bread
                or nothing at all,
                fasting nine days
                like the marathon monks of india

                      zafu pillow sitters
                      in white mountain galaxies,
            starry night sky constellation in my heart

        Run down by the river
        naked chest,
        hard and brown.

                whistling girls—
                hopscotch girls
                laying amongst the wildflowers and bees
                singing in the grass
                      purple vairochana,

                      the wildest of them all.

Today, Samuel, color pencil artist on the street,
        "I'm doing this here,
        for thirteen dollars,

>   because in town
>   I cannot find a place to sit—"

Today, Terry, soft spoken mumbler
> in Hunter Thompson sunglasses
> yellow mesh hat dirty and bent
> from Spokane, Washington—

>   "It's not a big city,
>   but it's a pretty good size city,
>   I think—"

Today, Jim, smelly red haired wing nut from Missoula
> who has existed twelve years
> on marijuana harvest rooftops
> in black tar hawaiian shirts,
> "Got spare change?"—
> *"No, man, sure don't."*

Today, Charlie, straw hat adolescent
> selling antique postcards for cigarettes
> and telling me this is my lucky day.

Today, Mike, ice beer drinker
> two week construction
> fall back alcoholic
>> buys groceries
>> and helps me carry the duct tape couch
>> for my porch.

Tonight, Margarette, ten years here
> Montana raised
> drunken hashish slur
> and slow to speak and pleasant—
>> sits on this porch,
>> bringing three baby kittens
>> and tells us their names—

>   twice.

Tonight, poorhouse redlight
> velvet district swingers,
> heavy ashtrays
> of piss yellow melted blown glass

spotted around the room

"GO!—" I yell loud.

"GO! GO!" bouncing back off the walls
        back at me
        or in the alley
        fast jazz snare

            golden horns
            ricocheting blue note
            cigarette smoke
            Chicago swing night madness

Stumbling orange man alcoholic
        on Malibu rum
        or White Russians—

            sunburnt and swollen
            through Yukon Jack
            Tequila Rose
            Brown bourbon
            and whiskey highs

"Who are you? and
            what's
                your
                    name?—"

Tell me, I say, tell me now
        and I'll leave you be,
        and come back next time
        with machine gun questions
        to clear your head

        then go about your way—

Rejoice! I say
          we're all alive and well
          looking for love,
              and kicks

                    or mahatma brown rice
                    for sale in the street

Rejoice, all you new age sadhus,
          burn your TVs
          and blow up your hairbrush,

          for I just found a dollar,
              beaten and torn,
              just found a dollar
                  in
                  my
                  bag.

Missoula coffee house o7.30.99

Early January Mountain Morning Frost

Jesus Bread Sandwich

What chew got?—
A Jesus Bread Sandwich?——
    and walked away.

Away with the sun
    blazing through the
    four—
    story—
    window

    and blinding me   —reflected
    off the flat oak table top——

A *Jesus Bread Sandwich*
    melting in the sun—
    and Holy Mountain Top
    melting in the horizon.

03.22.99 Chicago

Bukowski and the West

"*Chinaski!..*" and I walked out.
This is it?   —Yes, this is it.
You saw it coming. *And my check?* It's in the mail.

Enough to take me outta the city.
Enough to get me into the mountains,
        along the freeways—
        not sputtering,
        but sailing smooth.
Hot snow treads
        whining at top speed
        into warm western night.

Up and down,
        And around—
        Again.

Up into the great
        expanse of pacific northwest sun.

And a girl on my mind—
A girl I took care of
        in my mind.
Or I would take care of again—
        given the chance———

        the Romance of it all—
        written word for word
        in Rousseauean prose
        on cracked, yellow,
        duct taped pages.
Pages that stay
        in my head.
Pages that spell out "Chinaski!.."—

        Henry Chinaski, this is it.
        You saw it coming.
        And I was gone.

o4.o7.99 West Loop sun, Chicago

Four Foot Snow

Inside the cabin—
        and four foot snow outside.
Quiet, now, here—
        and four foot snow outside.

Wondering on the trail—
        three months of trail—
        and four foot snow outside.

Warm wool socks on my feet—
        and four foot snow outside.

Hot drinks
        to warm my insides,
        in my belly.
Hot, oriental rice,
        mahatma brown,
        and indian spices on the stove—
        and four foot snow outside.

Midnight, now, and handmade
        paper books from Nepal,
        Buddhist words inside
        fill the pages
        to fill my head—
        and four foot snow outside.

Sleepy dog on the couch,
        covered with blankets of wool,
        and cotton,
        with drips of snow on the carpet
        from his paws—
        and four foot snow outside.

Work on the mountain tomorrow,
        in cold winter december sun,
        and wind of nothing numbing my face.
Leather boots on my feet
        to keep me dry—
        in four foot snow outside.

But now— my bed——

Warm bed with heavy blankets—
        and a pillow soft as feathers,
        filled with feathers
        for me to dream and float about
        until the morning comes—

        and time to go
        out into the morning darkness,
        with frosty, pre–dawn breath
        in the early, moon–lit sky——
        reflecting back on my four foot snow outside.

12.20.98 Redstone, CO

Midnight Capital Limited

Midwest Midnight train–hopper madness.
Clickety–clack,
clickety–Cl——
WHAM!
       like a sonic blast out of ink black darkness
       and yellow lights out yonder across some field
       light the way and distance
            of steel
            engine
            airplanes
            going home,

Mindless passengers with ninety pound luggage
       and shopping bags full of retail sale racks
       and credit card blues,

Late night convicts
       laughing and slurring
       over beer can memories and poison cigarettes,
We may die tonight he says—

"I'll cut off my hair
       I'll sell it to the ladies of the night and travel to the Orient
       of silk opium laziness
       and Majarishi in zafu pillow meditation galaxies—"

Wailing headphones
       across the seat, bouncing head beat—
       no sleep for you, uptown, around town junkies of the streets

       Riding back and forth,
       clickety–clack along the tracks on this howling machine
            on a blissful–
                peaceful
                    American night.

ATL bound o4.27.99

Time Travel Train

...but sometimes I like to just sit and watch
in early-morning laziness
> with wet hair
> and sleepy eyes
out the window,
> bumping along, clicking.

As the clean suburban cookie-cutter houses with manicured lawns
turn to cracked neighborhoods and old-school barrios
> of the city.

Clicking by just in time to see the hermanitos on their way to school.
> Some running.
> Some playing.
> Some fighting—

screaming Walmart schoolbags swinging wildly
with reflective plastic-embroidered Saturday morning cartoons
> on the front.

Next stop, Western Avenue—
and my neighborhood begins to fade into burned-out forgotten brick
and crumbling wood of the factories and abandoned warehouses
that sit there, old and tired as a backdrop for the wandering eyes
> that bounce along
> on a time travel train.

o4.12.99 Chicago

Unemployed

Holy, holy, holy,
    Holy, holy, Holy

Holy, Holy, holy
  Holy, Holy, holy—
  Holy, Holy, holy—

HOLy, Holy, Holy—
    Holy, hOl—y, Holy
Holy—, HO——ly, HoLy
    holy....holY, hOly

hOLY Hholy—yYholy,
    OLYhe HhoilyyYholy

OµKYhe H¥oilfy! Yåçly
    OµKYhe **H¥oilfy!** Yåçly

OLYhe HhoilyyYholy
    OLYhe HhoilyyYholy

holy....olY, hOly
    Holy, holy, HoLy
    Holy, hOly, Holy

HOLy, Hol—y, Holy
    Holy, Holy, Holy—
Holy, Holy, Holy—

Holy, Holy, Holy
    Holy freedom.

o5.28 (again)

Mountain Girl

I saw you in the warm, orange light of a midnight bonfire,
but you didn't know, in warm winter sunshine air
with a sunburn on your face—

Sunburning your hair
making it lighter and straighter and more wonderful to see.

and more wonderful I'm sure—
to touch. but I didn't.

I saw the sun
shining in your eyes—
                              shining eyes,
more angelic than the mountain itself. and much sweeter to see.

You've been to Virginia by the beach
       with low, cold east coast waves
           bashing on the sand.
Salty sand   and late–night,
   early morning bonfires at high tide.
Smell of sandlewood burning,
       beer cans laying around
          and music quiet under the surf.

What about Montana?—
        ever go?—Vermont?—
New Mexico and to the hot springs of Arroyo Hondo
       Rio Grande cool clean winter sun and purified air
       for your long, blond hair and sunlight on your face
       and the mountains in your eyes,

       and the mountains in your eyes.

o1.o3.99 Marble, CO

Randolph Street

Early morning big city madness.
And a thousand cars
    screaming by rattle and jolt over steel–rimmed
sewer drains, and cracked, crumbling West Loop streets.

Buses with loud exhausts
that fill the air,
    and feel poisonous inside my lungs.

Roadside now drinking train station coffee—
    large, cream and sugar and mixed up
    with lazy, unused parking meters
    and red–brown brick reaching not as high,
        but as long
    as iron–rimmed man made   glass frame scrapers
    outlining the horizon.

Buildings that linger and hold back the sun—
    the sun that comes up and over
    bouncing off wet, oil–stained blacktop,
    reflecting back at me.

    Back on me. And my train station coffee.

Hot   train   station   coffee

and the morning sun on my face.

o3.17.99 Chicago

Far Off Places

Here Fly

Here I am to sit
        in the sun
With cap–sized,
        cut–off denim
        and dirt on my face.
Crazy, everywhere ants
        crawl up my feet
        and attempt a summit
        at my knees—
        they hardly ever make it.

The flys here at eight thousand feet are slow.
Like their grounded cousin the ant,
        they too find some need
        for my knees.

Not for long, though.
I shoo them away
        and away they go,
        slowly.

        Shoo, fly,

        shoo.

06.26.98 Bogan Flats Camp, Marble, CO

Daikensho Days

Educated glow inside
        that reaches for the sun
Lays down low
        and rests with me
               when I know my day is done.

With the sun it rises fast
        to start out every day—
        to glow from there,
        reaching out
        and teaching me the way.

Bodhidharma way of life
        to live the way I should—
        Daikensho in the city lights,
        Daikensho in the woods.

The grandest test that I have seen,
        from the grandest glowing eyes
        is a test of will
        that she will pass
        of the grandest size.
Instant karma tells me that
        figured that out as I sat
        on this train–ride
        misty–morning side rail.

Bodhidharma mystery.
        and my wool hat
        keeps me warm.
Warm inside so I can pass it on.
Warm inside to keep you strong.
Warm inside to keep me strong,

These days
        of circumstance are strange—,
        so don't cry, baby,
        don't cry.

o1.29.98 Chicago

The Big Question

Hospital pants,
Red *fruit–of–the–loom*
        thrift store t–shirt—
Tye–dyed socks
        with holes,
        or no socks on my feet.

Blue velour,
        outstretched softness,
Blue flannel bed clothes—
        based on the series you wore
        when you were six.

The kind that slide
        up to your knees
        as soon as you slide your legs under the covers,

        but you leave it
                or fix it—
        and feel better.

And wait for sleep
        and wonder what
        you'll wear—

        tomorrow.

02.16.98 Our kitchen

Warhol's Number

Last night I had a dream
        of Andy Warhol
        and me in his studio.

I showed him
        hot pink highlights
        of his blue velvet portrait.
He'd never seen this before
        and for him it was a first.
Thin, translucent
        tracing–like paper
        with those hot pink lines—
the contrast is what he loved.

He needed money,
        so I gave him some.
I asked him to sign what I had created,

but he signed using a number—
        a number I cannot remember—

        in pencil, in the lower right hand corner
        of the blue velvet portrait.

o5.28.97 Chicago

Route 200 East

I came across a road today
        called Desolation Row.
The trees were dead, the sun was gone,
        there was no wind to blow.

Dust and dirt and skulls of cows,
        ten buzzards in the sky,
the desolation hung so thick
        no bird could dare to fly.

The drive itself on wheels of stone
        through black and white terrain
left me grey and cold inside
        I couldn't stand the pain.

The hills on either side of me
        were formed of barren clay
the heat soared up to one–o–five
        and hotter in the shade.

Then I crossed a silver lake
        cold waves slapped on it's shore
the only sign of life around
        for a hundred miles or more.

So where then is the life that comes
        from Mother Nature's tears—
I'll dig some roots and plant a seed
        I guess it could take years

But, when I return, this place will have
        trees from east to west
the birds will sing and incubate
        blue eggs up in their nest.

And all because this lake stood by
        for something green to grow—
that once was known for miles around
        as Desolation Row.

o9.20.97 Montana highway

4WD

I really could use four wheel drive in my truck.

—pack in all my stuff and drive right up
    those crazy, bumpy,
    Rocky Mountain paths, to camp

        and see the stars
        from way out there.

06.26.98 Bogan Flats Camp Marble, CO

Double Door Inn

Neon lights that fill my room
borrowed fast from a yellow moon.
Harvest moon—coming soon,
Stay up late, and wait till noon.

And full music that fills my head,
from southern towns—
>South.
>Louisville.
>Memphis.
>Nashville.
>Hot 'lanta town.

Absolute Atlanta.
>Absolute fun.
>Absolute family,
>>take it and I'll run.
No time for fallacy,
No time for games, facades or pulling reigns
>of strung-out blondes
>that have no name,
>but play that tempting game.
>And feel the same.
And I'll tell you what they don't feel
I'll tell you what they don't know is real—

>>Real over big-breasted velvet-clad bar room singers,
>>Real over smoke-dained, rare-entifity fad,
>>Real over high school drop-outs
>>Real over feeling bad,
>>>feeling sad,
>>>And one more drink makes me glad
>>>to be here alone
>>>without the full-breasted Julia vocalists
>>>>with a smile all her own
>>>>and a hand-shake of rose.
>>>And Thomas Jefferson
>>>>on the crazy dollar bill that she looks for.

Here it is, under my shoe once more.

And here comes the moon.
Front–stage center and soft–magenta velvet dresses
    will help me sleep
       in the looney bin, of the wonderful city.

4:11 a.m., o2.o7.98 Chicago

Daikensho in the City, Daikensho in the Woods

American Road Prose & Highway Dharma

The Year I Changed the Royal Guard

There was a time when I checked out
        of that used up town of mine—
My family split—
        my house was robbed—
I took it as a sign.
So off I went to find a place
        that I could call my home—
All it seemed that I would need
        was my toothbrush and a comb.

Shoved them in my pockets
And started on my way—
        crossed the Caribbean Sea
        and desert in a day.

When I looked up and saw the road
        that wound around and out of sight—
I'd take off down that road at dawn
        and use the natural light.

And when it came I grabbed my comb
        and drug it through my hair—
        that night of slumber on the ground
        put tangles everywhere.

I hit the road and came across
        a bridge that span a moat—
        and flags that snapped—
        and old– gray poets reading what they wrote.

And when that drawbridge fell
        upon that rocky green terrain
The first time in my life I knew
I'd never be the same.
Stilted clowns with fiery sticks
        that twirled around the air—
        screaming frogs and pink go–tees—
        and women with no hair.

I wondered where they came from
        and the jester tugged my shirt——

It's all we've got— my strange— new friend
the king treats us like dirt—
I try all day to make him laugh but it never seems to work—
He throws his food and spits it at the maidens with a smirk——

So I went in to state my claim and see what I could do
When Johnny Cash was up on stage singing *Boy Named Sue*.
I knew right then that I would stay because you cant go back—
when he plays the first few notes of I'm the *Man in Black*.

So here I am to fill my day
with anything I choose—
and watch the jester live a life
of gambling, chicks, and booze.
I played the Queen in Aces
and took the King in pool—
the Jester brought me cocktails,
I took his kid to school.

As years rolled by and seasons changed,
I climbed the royal ladder—
the prince left town—
the court fell ill—
that King did just get fatter.

The food was served
       on plates of gold—
       and he always ate the most—
       he started first
       and finished last—
       No manners for a host.

The ducks were steamed
       and chickens plucked—
       and pie to feed the world—
       He ate it all and drank the wine
              and eyed the little girls.
And after that he'd smoke his pipe—
              finest tobacco in the world—
       the Queen would scream—

You see whadd–I mean?!—As her pearls began to shake—
You're doing yourself in, my love, and it's more than I can take!—

—I'm rich and young and run the world, don't tell me what to do!—

With that he screamed and grabbed his chest—
his face turned awful blue.

The court went nuts and I got up
and ran to pump his chest—
all I could do was kick his gut
and squeeze his head—
didn't know the rest.
But what the hell he's fat and old—
meanest man around
Don't blame me,
       it's not my job
         just 'cause he wears a crown.
And that was it— his final meal
        of meat and bread and wine—
        tell the people not to fear
        'cause I was next in line.

That crown was huge
       the robe didn't fit
       and the Jester was my friend—
Old man drank straight bourbon warm—
       and me an Irish blend.
But I was King and did my job
       and ran that hillside well—
       you should have heard the children laugh
       and stories I did tell.

For every night the bands would play,
       and food and land for all—
       no one poor,
       no one sick,
       the peasants had a ball.

That's how it was with me in charge
       with my new Queen right by my side.
The guards got paid, but did no work
       'cause my gates were open wide.
Everybody laughed and talked
       and camped out every night—

You know how it's done, our King, You really do it right!—

*But you all don't have to call me king—
we're all the same 'round here—*
>the farmers farm,
>the minors dig,
>and the brewers mix the beer.

And no one seemed to cry or mourn
>about that fat, old King,

Except that lonely Queen of his
>and all her diamond rings.

But she got old and used her gold
>on wine and jewels and rent
>and before that year was long past gone
>her fortune was all spent.

But I was King,
>my wife was Queen—
>we took that old wench in
>we gave her everything she needs—
>the Bishop took her sins.

And we stood by as months rolled past,
>saw her through her final meal
>of rice and wheat and cornish hens
>and silver–platter veal.

And when that hillside was truly mine
>and royalty all gone—
>we had a party went all day
>and lasted all night long.

The peasants laughed
>and I did too—
>they weren't peasants anymore—
>for all the gold that old king had
>was tossed out on the floor.
>We all took just enough
>to keep our families fed—
>and water warm
>and roofs from leaking the rain upon our heads.

There we stayed and slept and played—
>all the bellies full.

The jester told me jokes all day
>till that kid came home from school.

And then one night
        the band we loved
        failed to show it's face—
So— I got up—
        the Jester too
        and we sat in it's place.
All the people sang and danced
        when the Jester hit his harp—
        he made it scream like I never seen
        that man sure left his mark.

The court joined in with all the horns—
I beat all the drums—
        my queen sang mean—
        the dogs howled out—
        I never heard such lungs.
Before that music ended
        we needed one thing more—
        the Bishop picked his six string up
        and wailed like none before.

That crowd went nuts—
        and I just grinned
        and realized what we'd done—
We're all we need—
        there's nothing else
        to keep us from our fun.

So we played and played
        till the moon was gone
        and the little red rooster crowed.
We cleaned our mess– and drank the rest—
        and all left stumbling home.

So that's our gig
        and every night we sit out on our land
        the music wails—
        and the people come
        to see our rambling band.

And when the town across the hill
        heard our music loud—
        they all came by with food and wine—
        and to the King they bowed.
My people laughed

and hugged them all
and explained to them the way—
*It's up to you— do what you want
to fill your everyday.*

We don't need no king around to
tell us reasons why—
*do what you do the best you can—
don't let one day slip by.*

And then they saw the way we lived
and questioned with a grin—
*Where on Earth you people from—
and how'd this all begin?*
My Queen stepped up to answer that
and told them with a smile—
*It's all been going on since we chose
to make our lives worthwhile.*

With that they had no questions more—
some took the time to think—
others laughed and joined our crowd
and poured themselves a drink.

I kissed my new Queen's lovely lips
and slapped the Jester's hand—

*It's time to go—
this restless crowd wants to hear our band.*

And on we played into the night
with fires all around—
the heavens shook and tombstones rocked
back and forth in the ground.

Our family doubled up in size
and the band grew up as well—
and every night we gathered up until the full moon fell.

And in the day we'd do our thing—
the life and love was grand—
the family grew
cause all we need—

is life

and love

and land.

11.28.96 Johnson, VT and Thanksgiving in CT
For Robbie Miller— the disco van and Arizona thrift store Las Vegas gambling 3–piece suits.

Remembered

I want to be remembered
    hard at work—
        hunched over in old jeans and t-shirt—
            soiled hands
            and dirt on my face—

Tousled, tangled hair on my head—
        pay no attention—
        so deep in thought
            and effort
                and concentration to no end——

A work of art at my feet.

08.29.99 Missoula, Montana

Western Haiku

Quiet and

Twenty miles south
a mystic rushing river—
        Jackson, Wyoming.

Sleeping Out

Howling wolves y coyotes
up high on black mountain loud—
        'good night to you as well.'

In Cotton

Open azure sky—
>handmade sweaters on a fence,
>for sale in New Mexico.

Flannel Shirt.

Gas–stop truck driver
sitting stiff, flatland benchtop—
>Texarkana sun.

Last Chance Before Sunrise

from the Telluride Daily Planet

Although I don't remember much more of it than the mammoth walls of snow towering over my head around the walkway near our house, I spent the winter of 1979 (like most fortunate six–year–olds) in the warmth and safety of my immediate family in the near northwest suburbs of Chicago. And when holiday vacation came from first grade that year my brother, two sisters, and our motley crew of working class neighborhood kids spent all of the few daylight hours we had using all our energy and concentration to dig the most mysterious and complex catacomb of snow tunnels we could possibly imagine.

This was all I could think of, twenty–one years later, in the San Miguel Mountains of southwest Colorado as I lashed the traction cables to the rear tires of my 1995 Ford pickup truck and, unknown to me at the time, turned the wheel north toward the mounting blizzard that had for the past several hours been suffocating Lizard Head Pass sitting ten thousand feet above sea level. The irony in this was not that I was headed straight into the worst snow storm I'd seen since that winter of seventy–nine, but that my sole reason for going at all was to visit my family, fifteen hundred miles away, in the same town I'd played in everyday from sun up till sun down, twenty–one years before.

The skies over the past week had been clear enough, as Rocky Mountain winters go, with crystal clear blue skies and high altitude sunshine so bright it'll make you feel closer to heaven than you already are. I thought about this, too, as I clamped the last cable onto the rear passenger side tire of my truck. I figured the light snow coming down would blow over as soon as we crossed the pass, like it did most days. Then, as I would descend past Telluride and Placerville, surely wouldn't need these blasted snow chains at all.

According to how I planned it, the early morning sun and confident azure blue skies would melt most of the snow left after the plows did their thing, leaving nothing but water–logged sand strewn haphazardly along the asphalt, wet and playing wind chime songs on the metal body and steel bumper of my truck. Then, as the day drew on, drying up the roads to the east, from the central Rockies all the way to Chicago— this I was certain of. And not certain out of naiveté or sheer hope. Certain out of four and a half years of cross country expeditions covering the entire puzzle that makes up the lower 48 United States. Coast to coast countless times. Border to border in every season and weather condition man is blessed with from Mother Nature herself.

Taking another luke warm slug of sugary coffee, two hours later, I realized my predictions soon seemed terribly wrong. Although the truck weighed more than it had probably ever, only because, once again, like a modern day gypsy it contained nearly everything I owned, and the chains were securely fastened the roads were not getting better as I moved on. They were getting worse. Treacherous curves saturated with a thick blanket of fresh, dry powder painting the Aspens and black rock a cottony layer of fresh white— absent of guardrails or death–trap prevention of any kind. My predictions were wrong—Horribly wrong—and only getting worse.

From what I could make of it, the sun seemed to be going down. Not that there was any sun at all over head, but it was getting even harder to make out anything more than ten feet away on the other side of the windshield.

I slipped back to 1979, in the street—my long underwear soggy with sweat underneath the one piece snowsuit my brother or some cousin had surely worn the year before. I remembered the holes we dug out there in the cul–de–sac—the giant hills of snow built up daily by the township's monster snowplow trucks. I remembered the blanket we layed over one of these holes, covered it with powdery snow, and called for the neighbor girl to come running— And she did, just as planned—like we saw in the movies or on *The Dukes of Hazard* on Tuesday nights in the family room when our Dad wasn't around. This girl went tumbling head first into the Hollywood trap and yelled for help because she couldn't get out. I thought about the endless hours of snow coming down. I remembered the wind storms picking up at night, close to bed time, or worse yet in the middle of the night blowing so hard out there like the roof was caving in, surely the windows were about to give away, come crashing in, bringing the trees and bushes with them. I remembered all this, at twenty miles an hour, squinting to see the road. I remembered all this like it was a dream. But mostly I remembered feeling small——

I continued on, dazed and hypnotized into the swirling cloud constantly blanking my view of the road even three feet, now, in front of the truck—Just keep your foot pressed on the gas, ever so slightly, I kept saying to myself—Right where it's at now, any faster— spinning off the road I go, any slower and I'll stop—Can't stop because I'm just gliding over the ice now as it is, fooling myself thinking even for a minute that I am in control, and if I stop I'll never get enough traction to start again— that is, if I could stop at all—(It's like that dream we all have once in a while, I thought, where you are being chased by horribly terrifying creatures or simply normal people out to cause you harm—deranged in some way—on your trail at full speed and you know they're there, you know they are coming straight at you full boar—but you cannot run. You *may* be able to walk—and in the worst of these dreams, as those bastards in high pursuit get closer and closer, you may only be able to *crawl*. Only this time it seems a bit worse, I went over in my brain, because it isn't a dream at all, and it's happening at ten thousand feet.)

Now I was unable to see the sides of the road at all. If there happened to be a guardrail, which was almost never, I could possibly get a faint reflection back from my headlights and judge the distance this way. Other than that, if I did go off the road at this point, I wouldn't know whether I was falling five feet or five hundred—until I stopped.

As I came to a slight upgrade I pushed the accelerator in to compensate for gravity slowing me down—And as if in slow motion, the worst I could imagine happened. The back end of the weighed–down truck violently kicked out to the left, spinning almost ninety degrees into the oncoming lane. I spun the wheel to correct it, only to cause the reverse effect, back around I went in the opposite direction, absolutely sure I was going over the edge—Backwards. This is it, I thought—This is how I'm going to go. This is the end. I heard an old man once say at a campsite in Wyoming maybe, or some truck stop in Texarkana south, how his friend some years ago had died *"with his boots on"*, by which he went on to explain meant he had died on the road—traveling across the United States one last time. The man said that is how his friend wanted to go, and had predicted for himself that indeed that is how it would happen. Apparently he was right.

    By some minor miracle, I righted the truck, or the truck righted itself, and I was headed blankly, numb with fear, and sweating straight north once again on the road, my heart exploding over and over deep in my chest.

    I am no longer in control of such things, I thought to myself—No longer in control of this truck I'd so far driven over a hundred and twenty-seven thousand miles—No longer in control of where I would end up tonight—No longer in control of anything, but my mind.

    Just keep the foot where it is, I kept hearing in my head. Sing a song. Think of something else, but two feet of quickly fading white line paint to the right of my windshield was all I could see. I thought I would surely slip into insanity at this rate, then soon slide off the road at top speed into the darkness and snow, and if I didn't die, I'd wake up in the morning wrecked and half frozen in the trees somewhere discovered by a passing farmer out for the early edition and some coffee in the morning sun.

    Just keep the foot where it is.

    The town was called Gunnison. I knew this because an ambulance from the hospital there went flying past me in the oncoming lane, through the thick clouds of wind and snow. I could have cried when I made out the first shack along side the highway on the south edge of town. Maybe I did. When I found the motel my brain was wracked with pain. It was purely something I had never felt before. Absolute concentration and focus for such a length of time mixed with adrenaline and the very real possibility of death. I think the duration of this condition caused my body to tire itself out— Mile after mile. It's a truly natural condition, but after so much, time tends to wear on you a bit. My heart hurt as well. Probably for the same reasons. My face was red and my hair was in a state of emergency and alarm. I had trouble standing up at first, to step out of the truck—I felt dizzy like I was going to faint. I slid across the parking lot. Surely I scared the desk clerk, who worked only evenings at the neon–lit Hollywood Motel. She didn't want any trouble. *Who are you?—What's your name?—Here's your room.* I took my key, and asked her where I should park— *Soon as the snow stops they start towing from there, better move it now, find a better spot—Might be your last chance before sunrise.*

To Order This Book or visit the Painting Gallery,
Please go to **Rhythm Mountain Studios**—

www.rmsart.com

forthcoming...

the String Cheese Diaries—
*American Stories, Dharma Notes, Gadabout Letters,
Highway Ramblings and Poems from Above the Tree Line*